LEXICON DEVIL

BIRDLAND SLIM

CONTENTS

MARCH 2018 – MAY 2021

COVER DESIGN INSIPRED
BY THE GERMS 1981 e.p.
"WHAT I DO IS SECRET"

1. A MEMORY OF LISTENING TO DARCY PLAY PIANO AT THE SOUP KITCHEN

Having lunch at the Marion
Soup kitchen
With my friend Darcy
We eat the simple food
Amongst the cities down and out
And when we are finished the wonderful
And simple meal
Darcy plays the old piano
In the corner
He just makes up the music
It is so wonderful
And I just sit there
In this place
Where the soul comes to rest
Where spirit cannot die
The end of the rainbow
The down and outers
Hanging on

Dream: I am in school walking through the hallways of college or highschool. I am looking for my class. I am there to write my final exams, but I have Not gone to class or read the books. I don't know where the classroom is. I have Quit school and began to drink. I'm worried my Mother will find out. I haven't Gone to school in a long time. I go to a wholesale liquor store and buy some booze From some men across a counter. It is early in the morning. The liquor store is open 24 hours. I wake up. I haven't had a drink in three months.

2.   THERE IS BUT ONE SONG

I have but one song
To sing
One note to mourn
This life with
And it is that my heart
Is filled with love
It spills over
And comes out from
My eyes
As tears
for their is no one
Who's open arms
Embrace my heart
From birth unto death
A single moon
On the lone prairie

3. TALKING TO MY DAUGHTER ON MY GRANDSON'S FIRST BIRTHDAY

It is beautiful to hear
Your voice
Even on the cell
All the way away in Yellowknife
Today is the birthday
Of my grandson
One year old today
And speaking to you
My daughter
Has made everything
Beautiful
In the world

- March 28/2018

4. ON SEEING HARRY MANX AT THE CULTURAL EXCHANGE CLUB

Harry Manx
Playing "A Little Cruel"
As I sit in my seat listening
Feeling experiencing enjoying
This master of slide guitar
A deep profound feeling
Resonating through my heart
Collecting my soul
In the tones of his sound
His blues healer voice
Here in this old club
Dust and cobwebs
Old stage worn wood
The audience mostly new retirees
Trying to look like they are still cool
A grey-haired woman talking to her friends
And looking just as lovely as can be
Sips a drink catching my eye
A smoke machine puffs out
Threads of grey silk against
Red lights
What a beautiful night
Here I am in the second row
Right up close to this master
"Standing in the pouring rain

Watching the house burn down"
One of the best the world has
What a lucky man
I am

      -April 27/2018
      Regina Cultural
      Exchange club

5. POUR

Writing poems
Sun shines in the window
Without some tea
I don't even feel like a poet
Alcohol and marijuana
I've put them aside
They once engendered all my words
But I need a new
Medium
The sun shines in the window
I pour tea into the cup

6.   I WAS SO CLOSE TO LOVE

But my hands could not reach it
And it fell away from me
And now my heart rests
In a pool of its own tears
The edge of sadness
Break my heart in two
Stand under the lone moon

Dream: I am in a desk in college or university. Next to me is the Master poet Irving Layton. He is listening to the professor give Her lecture. He is smiling and nodding his head. I can't believe it.

I'm right next to the great Irving Layton. I can't even imagine speaking To him, so I begin to write a poem about the event, then I am in another Room With Harry Manx and we are playing guitar together. Harry Manx Is impressed with my playing. I can't even believe it. June/2018.

7.   HAPPINESS CAN ALWAYS BE YOUR BEATING HEART

Happiness can always be yours
Like that sun there in the sky
Or that cloud that's floating
Right above you
Happiness can always
Belong to you
Love can always be received
Like the beating of your heart
And the blink of your eyes
Happiness can always
Be yours

-July/2018
For Sally

8. EARLY MORNING

8 o'clock Sunday morning
Having coffee
Listening to Richie
Ramone On Facebook
"There are kids living on the street
Just looking for something to eat"
Lol
I send a text to a poet
I know in Moscow

-August/2018
For Vera Drozdova

9. DAKHABRAKHA AT THE REGINA FOLK FESTIVAL

Regina Folk Festival
Lovely people sitting in their chairs
On stage come three tall black hats
With black dresses
And a bald man with a beard
They begin to play
Beautiful music, Ukrainian music
I went down to the stage
To watch them
Wow
I had never heard of them
They are from Kyiv
And I bought their C.D.

-August/2018

10. BRUCE COCKBURN – REGINA FOLK FESTIVAL

Beautiful day
Here I am standing near the stage
Watching and listening
To Bruce Cockburn
At the Regina Folk Festival
One of Canada's greatest musicians
Wonderful crowd
Beautiful music
Grey-sky overhead
Veiw of city hall
Over the roof of the stage
And Bruce Cockburn plays
His beautiful music
"If I Had Rocket Launcher"
On a steel guitar
Everyone is dancing and smiling
And having a great time

-August/2018
Victoria park
Regina

11. DYING THE POETS WAY AS SEEN THROUGH THE POOR CLOSED EYES OF THE DREAMER

When poised with death
Waiting there
The road has to turn away
Hoping not to die alone
Never to find
That angel of the heart
Broke alone and dying
In the gutter
The bottle of booze
Spilling in the street
The poets way

September/2018

12. IN A DREAM A POET SPOKE TO ME AND I DIDN'T ANSWER FOR I HAD NOTHING TO SAY

I want to sit as a poet
In the University
In a beautiful wood lined room
Look out the window
Watch the leaves fall in autumn
Smoke a pipe
In my tweed coat
Look at the young people
Wearing autumn coats
Working for their degrees
Moving towards their lives
And old poet
Enjoying the day, light
And air
But, I'm just here
In this old house
Long from all that
Could this mean anything to me
No one knows my name
Just a coffee for my drink
And just music for my friend

September/2018

13. REMEMBERING LI PO

What to do now with my life
That so much has passed
And so much didn't come
True at all
I see all the mistakes
Laid before me in
A necklace of tears
So what?
And who cares anymore
Defeated in life
And what now shall I do?
Trying not to break the glass
Trying to embrace the reflection
Of the moon
In the dark river

-October/2018

Dream: I am at a theatre in London. A play is being performed on stage. I'm a stage hand or something. I'm backstage. The Smiths are performing Next. It is their first ever gig. Morrissey is lying on a couch in a dark blue shirt, Big hair. He seems totally at ease and Johnny Marr is sitting with his guitar On a low stool. The only time I ever met the Smiths in a dream. October/2018

14. IF I ONLY HAD TWO HANDS TO LEND THEN YOU'D SEE WHAT A FRIEND MEANS

Going down this lonely road
For so long
I don't see no end
A rag tag poet
With the money always running out
Drowning in the burden
Of alcoholic debt
How is love
To place its long arms
Around me
When tomorrow wants
Payment on its sun
And even the "friends"
Have no hands to lend

15. WAKING FROM THE ALCOHOL DREAM

My soul
Empties itself of the booze
My ramblin' head
And the cold sidewalk
Closing down to a year
The moon seems
So lonely in the sky
Without its drunken broken-hearted friend
And all the girls at the liquor store
Wonder where there constant boy
Has gone
Waking up from the
Alcohol dream Morning and sun
And just an empty road there

-November/2018

16. SQUEEZE IN THE GOOD

Sun breaking in the window
Listening to Bob Marley
Having a coffee
Cold snow over the yard
Gotta take the good with the bad
Squeeze that good in
With the bad
There's always some good
Even when the sun
Refuses to shine
And tomorrow
Wants its payment up front
And all the corners
Are closing in

-November/2018
Regina

17. BIRTHDAY

Long away
And far ago
We once met each other's eyes
And today you
Sit 'round somewhere
Family and cake
Today is your birthday
And I am here
Reading "A Junkies Christmas"
By William S. Burroughs
And now our eyes
Are as far apart
As sun and moon
And it is just another day
The broken-heart of yesteryear
Payin' down its debt
Of tears
To the goddess of love
I puzzle at this long ago
Dream
And was ever love
Ever real
Or just a poem in a book
Not sanctified by any fate
Or degree of time

-December 13/2018

18. MILE

And here I am reading
"A Junkies Christmas"
By William S. Burroughs
From "Interzone"
A book I bought in Toronto
July "90
We were to get married that summer
But, things never did work out
For us
And you went to B.C.
To visit your cousins
And I went to Toronto
Alone
And I bought this book
At a big bookstore downtown
And now today you turn 50
A long solar system
Away from me
How could I have for seen this day
Way back then
This day
Today
You with all your sunflower brightness
And I'm here alone
Waiting for the poet to empty
His cask of wine

To free this broken heart
So long lost
So long ago

    -DECEMBER 13/2018

24

19. PETE SHELLEY HAS DIED TODAY

Peter Shelley has died today
Frontman of the Buzzcocks
Legendary Manchester punk band
The most intelligent of the punks
Unbelievable guitar riffs
Sad eyes crying over the news
I still have the old album
I bought back in '81
Spend your time
Running free
Run free
Peter Shelley

-December 16/2018

20. OLD BUZZCOCKS RECORD

I put my old Buzzcocks record
By the stereo system
In honour of Peter Shelley
Who has died
The record is old and frayed
But it is still new to me
I realize I've owned it for almost
40 years
And the record seems old
Like Mom and Dad's old records
An artifact from the past
Long ago and far away
Time has changed
I was in highschool then
And now I'm over 50
And Pete Shelley is dead
And my old record
Sits by the stereo
Time has gone by

-December 16/2018

WHY SHE'S A
GIRL FROM THE CHAINSTORE
STRANGE THING
RUNNING FREE
BUZZCOCKS

21. I CAN'T HELP IT IF I'M STILL IN LOVE WITH YOU

Anita Carter and Hank Williams
Singing together
Looking at Anita's beautiful eyes
And smile
As she Looks at Hank Williams
you can read every emotion
On her face
Singing together on this black and white
Video on Youtube

"and I can't help it if I'm still in
love with you"

So lonely here by myself
And I wonder where you are
And I can only sit here alone
And wonder where you are
I got no drink in my hand
I left that behind on this lonesome trail
And your memory
Is a ghost that haunts me
From my heart

And I can't help it if I'm still
In love With you

-January/2019

22. I LOST MY MIND

When the crash came
I lost my mind
And then the booze took over
The plan
Crashing and burning
Through it all
Until there was nothing
Left
And now
Even the booze
Is gone

-January/2019

23. DOWN TO THE BLUES

Down to the blues
Jimmie Dawkins "Hard Life Blues"
Sitting on a Friday night
With Youtube
"Cold as Hell"
No bottle of booze
Feeling the pain
Of the blade edge
Against the breaking heart
Down to the blues
And the night is cold
The snow is hard
And nothing good
Is in sight
Down to the blues
Down to the night
Even the moon laughs
From its place in the dark sky

-January/2019
Regina

24. OLD BOOKSTORE

Entering the bookstore
Piles of old dusty books
On the wood shelves
Darcy once sold them
Some books he had
He had stolen from the Food bank
So we could get enough money
To buy some dope
I buy what I could only call
A treasure
A book of poems by
Earle Birney
How nice

-February/2019
Centennial mall
Regina

25. THE FLOYD

Listening to Pink Floyd
"Alan's Psychedelic Breakfast"
On Youtube
Drinking some tea
It is not breakfast time
But, late at night
But, that's ok
Its always morning
Listening to the sunrise
Of "Alan's Psychedelic Breakfast"

26. COLD WINTER TRAIN BRIDGE

Freezing cold outside
Hard snow
Driving downtown
Passing beneath
The iron train bridge
A big cargo train
Rattles quickly by
A man in his 50's
Thinking of his lost loves
And broken hearts
All that was pulled from his grasp
Never to lodge in his
Memory
Cold winter loneliness
No open arms to run to
And my poor only job
May not even last

-February/2019

27. "IN SOME HIGHSCOOL YEARBOOK THERE ARE POEMS AS BEAUTIFUL AND REAL AS THE EYES OF YOUR LOST LOVE"

There's kids who've written better stuff
For their Highschool yearbooks
Then some of the things I've penned
Well away, immortal ink drips
Hardly from the tip of my pen
And old Pound had but to write
Of the Italian Campagna open road
A little tobacco shop
And the lady who was his sargasso sea
Date his poems from Paris
And then down to the ship
And me
I labour this some 30 years
Bent upon ringing
Lillies from acorns
Succeeding
At best scribbling some lines
With the value of nothing

28. TICKETS FOR MORRISSEY IN SASKATOON

The blue YMCA towel
Making a shadow on the wall
Of Morrissey's profile
His pompadour hair and lantern jaw
I smile as I read a book
And yes I have tickets
To Morrissey
In Saskatoon
And this will be so wonderful
To see this man
Who changed my poor only
Life forever
And saved my life
A thousand times
Morrissey
In Saskatoon
Seems like a crazy
Dream

-February/2019
Regina

29. SITTING WITH MY FRIEND RIC AT THE HOCKEY GAME

Freezing ass cold
Going to the good'ol hockey game
Regina Pats vs. Kootenay Ice
I park my Toyota in the cold
Parking lot
And head to the orange topped
City hockey arena
Where the Regina Pats play
You can smell the popcorn
And the ice
Hockey fans milling about
All kinds of people here
Hockey fans
I walk the concourse
Look up as I always do
At the Memeorial cup banners
I watch the teams
Warm-up on the ice
In my usual spot
The players skate by in circles
Shooting pucks at the Goalie
I buy a hot dog and a coke
And go sit with my friend Ric
We talk about the Pats
And the Roughriders

And memories of trips
To Los Angeles and Disneyland
What are sons are doing
We watch the game
Discussing the goals
Pats win tonight
5-2 in a great comeback
Beating the odds
I jump into my frozen car
The night is cold

-February 20/2019

30. ON SEEING CARMANAH AND OCIE-ELLIOT AT THE ARTESIAN

Cold cloudless night
The Artesian club
a light outside the door
Shoveled snow
Up the stairs and into
The club, which was once a church
What a beautiful room
Shiny wine coloured cloth
Hanging at the back of the stage
I sit down alone
By a hipster family
The opening band Ocie-Elliot
Are getting their equipment
On stage-just two people
A man and a skinny
And beautiful lady
Carmanah is back there
On the road
Broken down in Brooks, Alberta
Ocie-Elliot play some beautiful
Harmonies
The skinny lady has a
Charming smile
And the guy has a Martin guitar
Carmanah gets here a bit late

The singer is beautiful
And skinny too
Dressed in black with a red scarf
And her dark hair in a bun
They tell us of their ordeal
Stuck on the frozen prairie
Getting their transmission repaired
in Brooks
And driving across the frozen
highway at night
To get to the Artesian
Their music is lush
And warm and beautiful
I could listen to them
All night
When the wonderful concert is done
I go home
In the star spangled frozen
Night

February/2019
Artesian club
Regina,Sask.

31.   MY POOR OLD CAT

I'm at the Vets office
Holding my poor old cat
In a blanket in my arms
 She fell from a tree
That a dog chased her up
And she broke her pelvis
And so I have to put her down
Its just a sad, sad thing
That rests there
In my arms
Its just sad
Its just a sad, sad
Thing

-April 5/2019
Regina
For Sox

32. ONE WEEK THE CAT IS GONE

When I hear a noise
I think its that old cat
Then I look around
And the cat isn't there
I think I better check the door
And see if the cat wants in
I miss my poor old cat
All the world was love
To her heart
And everyday was beautiful
To her

-April/2019

33. WAITING FOR MORRISSEY

Well, that bastard Morrissey
Rescheduled from April to October
A proper wait I guess
To see my legendary muse
Well, I'm waiting for the autumn
Waiting for Morrissey
Waiting in the eventful gloom
The hollow hatful
The everyday is like Sunday
Waiting

-April/2019

34. THE FUNERAL OF BOB MARLEY

Watching the funeral procession
Of Bob Marley on Youtube
Its 2019
I remember back when this happened
But, I had never seen
All the people standing along
The road
As Bob's funeral truck
Passed by
Beautiful
The colours of the video
Are faded and grainy now
That was almost 40 years ago
Technology was really primitive then
Time passes and splits
In a second
Its 1981
But, here I am
53 years old now
Looking backwards in Time
On Youtube
And though it was almost
40 years ago
I sit here
Eyes with tears
Seeing all the people

Who loved him
Lining the roads of Jamaica
To see their favourite son
Into eternity

    -May/2019
    Regina

35. LEARNING STOMPIN' TOM CONNORS "THE HOCKEY SONG" ON GUITAR

Setting down to it
Learning Stompin' Tom's classic
Canadian song
"The Hockey Song"
On my Epiphone guitar
The chords seem simple enough
But getting it right
Is not quite so easy
I watch the Youtube video
The leafs are playing the L.A. kings
Jacques Plante walks past the camera
Onto the ice
"Someone roars
And Bobby scores"
Indeed
Praise be
For 'ol Stompin' Tom

-May 2019

36. YOUTUBE

I'm watching Lynn Anderson
"I Never Promised You a Rose Garden"
On Youtube
Beautiful song
"Come on and share the good times
while we can"
Then I look in the comments
And a man writes that he loves and hates
this song
That his Father played
It all the time back in the day
The song was playing on his 8-track
In his car
Before he left for Vietnam
And was killed
His last words
"I love you son"

-May/2019

37. PERHAPS, ONLY...

Perhaps, only
Other poets
Will understand
These small rays
Of light
I have made for
you
Perhaps, Only
Lovers and loners
And the wanderers of sorrow
Wiil understand these words
As the beginning of dreams
Of destinies
Perhaps, only…

38. MORRISSEY-TCU PLACE-SAKATOON

Well, here I am
In Saskatoon
I drove up here to see
Morrissey
in all his non-cancelled glory
I park several blocks down from the theatre
And walk down to the city center
When I take my seat there is a screen
On the stage and music is playing
And pictures of morrissey
Are on the screen
Morrissey was so great
When I first heard him in the Smiths
Just at the end of school
He completely changed my life
And gave me direction in my poetic
Vision
Not a lot of people here
When Morrissey takes the stage his first words
Are "Tonight is not cancelled!"
And breaks into song
He plays the classic songs
"Everday is like Sunday"
"How Soon is Now"
"The Queen is Dead"

A man dressed like a Morrissey clone
Jumps on stage
And gives Morrissey a hug
And Morrissey tears his shirt open
During the encore
He starts a last song
Then cuts it short and leaves the stage
Morrissey plays Saskatoon
I leave the theatre and drive back to Regina
The sky is dark
And my heart is filled with joy
At seeing Morrissey
My poetry hero
Alive and in person
I play his music all the way
Down the dark highway

-October 22/2019

39. AND I RAISE THE FLAG BEFORE
   THE BRAVE

Not in the conscious
                    of the time

Nor even in the center of
A glacier valley filled with
Blue flowers
Will you find the love
That I had
To give
            To you

…..not in the consciousness
                    Of the Times
Nor even

                    -for Kenneth Patchen
                    The finest poet
                    In the U.S.A.
                    In times not
                    that Long ago

                    -November/2019

40. OUTDOOR HOCKEY –
FOOTBALL STADIUM

There's snow coming down
In the big football stadium
Home of the Saskatchewan Roughriders
But, today I'm here
To see the Regina Pats
Play outdoor hockey against the
Calgary Hitmen
I've got a great seat
The wind is blowing
And the snow is coming down
In large swirling flakes
Its cold
Its beautiful
I love it
What a wonderful day
Outdoor hockey in the cold I have a coffee
Sitting beside me is a friend
Of my buddy Ric's son
We got tickets together by accident
So nice
We talk throughout the game
Its fun to watch the Pats play outdoor
hockey Everyone seems so happy
The final score doesn't even seem important

Its just a lovely day
For hockey

    -October 27/2019
    Mosaic stadium-Regina

52

41. ROCK N ROLL

Rock n' roll destroyed America
And dragged the western world
Down with it too
And so beget the story
Of my life
The tale of an ordinary man
In no place
Doing nothing special
At all
But, I was dragged by the wind
Across the prairies
To look up
At a grey luminescent moon
And to dream of the sun
And the warm embrace
Of a beautiful day

-January/2019

42. 54ᵗʰ BIRTHDAY

It is my 54th birthday
And my heart is still broken
Over you
All day your arms embrace another
In my melancholy dream
I loved you
I love you so much
I've lived my life without you
What am I supposed to
Do?

-January 12/2019
Regina

43. LET US DRINK NO MORE

Let us drink no more
 For lost tomorrows
Let us drink no more
For sad memories of yesterdays
Let us drink no more
For our wayward illusions
And the ghosts of our minds

Let us drink no more

44. "A FEW DROPS OF TIME"

A few drops of time
To spend with you
A few drops of memory
To connect with you
Your voice long away
In Medicine Hat
But, that's just fine
There is sun in the sky
And there is no rain
Anywhere
Talking to you

       -for Angie D.
       My Medicine Hat gal
       -Title from Jean-Paul Sartre

45. READING SARTRE AGAIN
AFTER 30 YEARS

Again I pick up
This old book
"The Age of Reason"
By Jean-Paul Sartre
I first read it back
30 years ago hot summer
1988
I was just a young fool
Back then
I read it outside in the heat
In the bathtub or under a tree
Never read anything like it before
I was just ready for love
Waiting to meet my future
Unrequited love
In the hot summer time
The future open before me
But now thirty years have gone by
And my love is long gone down
the highway
And I am not young any more
So many plans
That never came true S
artre's the age of reason
What does that mean?

MONTAGE FOR AN INTERSTELLAR CRY
ANDREW SUKNASKI
HIRAETH
POEMS BY
Carol Rose Daniels
LOVERS AND LESSER MEN
new canadian library original no6
the poems of earle birney
a new canadian library selection

46. "THESE USELESS GIFTS"

Poetry has returned
Only these useless gifts
My broken heart
And my unrequited love
Your beautiful green eyes
Your beautiful brown eyes
My blue eyes ever crying
In the rain
A heart that is as empty
As a cloud
Here I am broken again
There is only this broken heart
And poetry
Leaves only these
Useless gifts

-November/2019

47. THE GHOST OF MY VERY SOUL

The ghost of my very
Heart
Entwined around this
Darkness
The memory fades
But my heart
Is still broken
And the light of the sun
Keeps coming, coming down
From the sky
Every day

-January/2020
Regina

48. MY UNREQUITED LOVE STANDS AT THE EDGE OF A DREAM

Trying to mend this broken heart
With the pieces of string
That I weave between us
 With these poems
I've written for you
I still see you there
In the balcony of my mind
And I am but a weakness
And a serial dreamer
A ghost
The memory of a ghost
A literary stalker

49. SONGS OF LONG AGO

Songs of long ago
In my heart I still
Remember you
how i felt the first time
I heard the songs
Singing the words
In my head
In the Highschool hallways
The people around me
And all the cute girls
And the clothes they wore
The teachers, the crushes
The heart broken dances
Now I can see these songs on youtube
Long gone are those days
Down the prairie fields
So nice to hear
These songs of long ago

-January/2020
Listening to the Ramones
On Youtube

50. I MUST LIVE WITH THIS BROKEN HEART

I guess I must live with this
Broken heart
Forever
An ephemeral shadow
In my own life
You are gone
Long ago down that road
And my heart is as broken
As it was the last time I saw you
Like yesterday
And how is this so
After an eon of time
And a river of booze
I'm still here
With this memory
Of you
And this broken heart

- January/2020

51. FOR ANGIE

My heart has eyes
And they will blossom sooner
For you
And there will just be sunshine
And blue sky
And just us two
Together

    -February/2020
    Waiting for April
    To visit Angie
    In Medicine Hat

52. LOOK YONDER AT THE POET HE HAS LEFT ONLY DEBTS

Enchanted by the light
In a pool of water
At midnight
My future a dark star
A distant myth
An old forgotten man
Holding only
In his hand
An orange
Flower

-March/2020

53. ALL THE BEAUTIFUL THINGS THEY PLACED LONG, LONG FROM HERE

My eyes
Crying tears
For the fool
That I always
Have been
A far away
Distant shadow
A silence

54. IN THE MIDST OF THE CORONA VIRUS

A heavy pallor
Hangs over the city
A paranoia in the heavy air
Everything is closed
No sports, no concerts
Never seen this before
In this life
Constantly on the news

-March/2020
Regina

55. IN THE MIDST OF THE WORLD'S FEVER

The lay-off notices began today
No work and the dole
Covid 19
Everything is closed
Everywhere

-1st day of spring
MARCH/2020

56. IT SEEMS AS THOUGH TIME HAS GONE LEAVING ME WITHOUT YOU

Going through these memories
From 30 years before
Sadness
Is all I can feel
Standing in these empty buildings
No face to see
If you want to know what happened to me
It is the same thing that happened to you

57. EVERYWHERE I SEE

The morning
That could have been
Everywhere beautiful moments
That never happened
A tear from one's eye
Is a broken dream
A shadow
A page torn from a book

58. STATE OF THE WORLD

A virus encircles the world
Here is empty streets
And death looms in secrecy
22 dead in Nova Scotia
From the gun of one man
And here I am
As the world revolves
Through nothing
And |I hold a ball of your memory
In my hand
Wondering

-April/2020

59. THERE IS NO TIME LEFT TO START AGAIN

But, lord have mercy there in the sky
That perhaps the new
Revolution of this earth
Will bring sunshine
And warm breezes
And everything wonderful
And happy
And here

60. IF ONLY I COULD TELL YOU

If only I could tell you
These stories
I see in my eyes
In the cinema of my mind
In all the details
Thread and bone
As I only lived it
If I only could have

61. COVID 19 IS SETTLING DOWN EVERYWHERE

When i go to the Ukrainian co-op store
I wash my hands and wear a mask
And I keep the distance
Masks on all faces
And the sun is shining
And today the sky is blue
They are rioting
Down in the U.S.A.
And covid is spreading everywhere
And its beautiful in my backyard
And the sun is shining
Anyway

62. ON SEEING BOBBY VINTON AT EXHIBITION PARK IN 1972

I saw Bobby Vinton
At Exhibition park
A million light years
Of time ago
I was there with my Mom
And my sister
I still remember Bobby Vinton
They had about three singers before him
And when he came out to perform
He was dressed all in sparkly white clothes
And white shoes
A lot of people there
In the horse racing park
And Bobby Vinton sang his songs
And my Mom was happy

63. THE POET WARNS OF COMING FAILURES AND SETS OUT TO PROVE THIS HIMSELF

The poets life
Is a great sadness
And a rare joy
And the poet's death
Will be his only
Crowning achievement
The only thing
He will be remembered
By

64. REGINA BEACH TRIP

Taking the highway to Regina Beach
Yellow canola like great sea waves
Driving down through the Lumsden valley
Horses and cows
Warm and beautiful in the sunshine day
Regina Beach is a buzz
With people
Everyone lazying around
But this is covid 19 times
Nobody cares at the beach
They are all celebrating life
On this beautiful summer day
A circle of muslim women around
What looks like a silver hookah
Or samovar
All dressed in black with gold and
white trim
Beautiful
Two men smoke from hookah pipes
Under a tree
Immigrants enjoying the afternoon
The Canadians showing off their trinkets
Of wealth
The smell of suntan lotion
And beautiful people

-July 11/2020

65. ONCE I WAS STANDING A LONG WAY FROM HOME

No one cares
That my mother loved me
Or that I once embraced the sun
Or cried tears beneath the lone moon
Indifferent like a great sea
Made from tears

66. INDIFFERENT LIKE THE GREAT SEA

Once I was standing a long
Way from home
There was no embrace there
There was nothing but a deep
emotion
My eyes
Were filled with tears
With only
A
lone
Moon
In
The
Sky

-July 16/2020
Regina

67. MEETING YOU IN THE BAR POLSKI

Your eyes are like
Two dark moons
And I forgot I was
In the bar Polski

-August/2020

Art work by Gek Sparrow

68. COVID 19 TEST

Today I got a covid 19 test
I went down to their testing station
For I was sick this week
There is no vaccination
Just two weeks quarantine
I waited in my car for my turn
I walked through the clinic of
masked people
They put a long q-tip into my nose
I began to worry about covid
What if I have it?
I could die
not a good feeling
At all

-August/2020

69. AND THE POET WANDERED ALONE
AS A BLUEBIRD SLEPT IN A TREE ABOVE

Where would the poet be
If he was not
A hopeless love-sick fool
What could the poet pen with a
heart not made
From Broken glass
And would the muse of poetry
Offer her glance
To poems penned
In joy and ease and wealth?
No
The muse of poetry
Only wants to see your heart
There before her
That is all she asks of you

70. A GHOST OF LOVE PEERS INTO YOUR EMPTY HEART

Maybe there is no love in my heart
Maybe there is a ghost there
A ghost of love
A passenger in my own life
A passenger in my own heart
I died a long time ago
And what has come by
Has been only a wait and a dream

I'm about thirty years old. Its late at night. I'm drunk and stoned. I take Ezra Pound's "Personae" for a drive to Regina Beach. The sky is filled With stars in the summer heat. I read some poems from Pounds book on The bench at the Bluebird Café' and on the pier. I drive back home to Regina. It is late at night.

71. POETIC HEART

If I could heal the broken
With my poems
And let my big poetic heart
Mend their soul
If I could do this
Then I could say perhaps
My life has not been entirely
In vain

-October/2020

72. MY MOTHER'S GOOD LUCK CHARMS

All my Mother's good luck charms
Could not help me in the end
I would keep on making
Poor choices
In my carelessness
In my weakness
And in my innocence
What was I except a disappointment
What was I except a shadow
And all this poetry I wrote
Is nothing at all

-October/2020

73. THE PEOPLE OF THE U.S.A. VOTED OUT TRUMP

On T.V. I saw in America
They have voted out Trump
And people are in the streets
Hugging each other in relief
There is joy on the streets of America
People are so happy

-November/2020

74. LOSING MY JOB AT THE YMCA DURING COVID 19

Well now I have lost my job
At the YMCA
As covid 19 closes down all
Layed off and gone
I am unemployed
And all I have before me
Is a lone bottle of alcohol
And a stunned memory
Of a time that is no longer here
And who will hire me now?
What can I do?
Will I lose everything?
My mind breaks like a shattered star
I don't have a job
What will I do?

-November/2020

75. LOSING MY JOB

So here I am once again
Alone and unemployed
A casualty of covid 19
Lord have mercy on my soul
who will hire me now that I am old
what will I do to pay these bills

76. POEM AFTER OSIP MANDELSTAM

I stand alone in the kitchen
The good smell of marijuana

Sharp knife big square brick of
Lancashire cheese
Pump up the heat all the way in the cold

And I will pace alone in the kitchen
drinking whatever I can to calm me down

And is there a station somewhere to find
So I can fly away from this forever

77. HAVING NO JOB DURING COVID 19

Here I am alone with no job
On this December day before Christmas
Covid 19 has brought itself upon the earth
And even the U.S. president was
brought down
By this world virus
And I am alone here
The air feels thin
The sun seems so far away
The light seems dim
And who's fault is it
The place I worked closed its doors
And out the door I went
And now I pace the house
Like a haunted hunted man
I have no job anymore
And if it wasn't for Sally
My English loveliness
I would have no support here
At all

-December/2020
Regina

78. UNEMPLOYED AND ALONE

I feel as though a man
Who moves each day closer
To the noose
On his execution day
Will the money run out?
Will my home go to?
What will tomorrow bring?
Does anybody know?
I pace the floors
Alone
What to do now
That the good job is gone
And nothing is on the horizon

79. WAITING TO HEAR ABOUT A JOB

Waiting hoping wishing for a new job
Waiting to hear from the employer
waiting for a call
Wondering what will unfold next
No power no control
Just waiting on someone else's words

80. CHRISTMAS DAY-NO JOB, NO MONEY, NO NOTHING

Christmas day
And I am unemployed
But hopeful
Will the new year bring
Glad tidings and joy
Or will it bring the crash and burn
I sit here alone
It is Christmas day
And I'm a shadow
A nothing
A man without a meaning

-December 25/2020

81. FACING THE END OF THE YEAR WITHOUT A JOB

The streets of Times square are empty
The New York city globe
Ready to drop
The covid fear
Haunting this the last day
Of the year
And I am alone
Facing the new year without a job
A bottle of booze and a sadness
Where will I be this time next year?
 I don't know

82. ON BEING OFFERED A JOB

I've been offered a job
To start in January
At the big mall
And I am happy
But my heart is filled with unease
just the same
It all seems so unreal
Tossed about on the sea
Washed ashore
The sun rising once again
over the earth

83. A POEM ON EZRA POUND

Listening to the recorded voice
Of Ezra Pound
On Youtube
A video spanning Time
To hear the old mesmerizer's voice
In this another century
It is like a voice
From another sphere
The poets voice
There alive for me to hear

February/2021

84. FOR THE POET 'S REJOICE IN THEIR DEATH FOR THIS WHEN THEIR LIFE BEGINS

To have been murdered by Stalin
In a gulag in Siberia
Is great on a poet's resume'
Or to die drunk and beaten
In a city gutter
Left there by thugs
Is a death poets dream of
Let every poet have the death
They wish for
The one they deserve
Alone
And withered to a thread
Their last ration
Left for the mice

85. IN A DREAM I WALK DOWN A LONG HALLWAY WHERE SYLVIA PLATH IS STANDING WITH A FORLORN LOOK IN HER EYES

In my dream Sylvia Plath
Sits in the chair
Of her eloquent mind
Holding an open book of poetry
In her hands
I look out a window
And the liquor store
Says "open 24 hours"
The dark skies begin to
Rain

86. TO BE A GENUINE POET ONE MUST BE OUTSIDE THE REALM OF POSSIBILITIES

I endeavored only to bring what
I had known

And saw and felt

Here in this life that I lived

I entertained no themes

I wrote for no journals

I wrote nothing to win a prize

I never thought anyone would
buy my books

I didn't write for the written page

87. COVID 19 VACCINATION SHOT

Drove out to the University
And had my Covid 19 vaccination
AstraZeneca
I drove out there
And the sky was overcast
I parked by the old gymnasium
And went inside
I talked to a woman and she told me
To go into the gym and wait at a table
A nurse came round and gave me my shot
And then I waited 15 minutes to leave
All good
Lots of people there
My arm started to hurt
But i was fine and doing my part

April/2021

88. A MAN WITH A CLOSED HEART

A man with a closed heart
Sits alone waiting
For the dissolving of Time
For the final ray of sunlight
Neither wanting to leave
Nor stay
Not wanting anymore memories
Having known beauty
And sorrow
And wanting only
Light and air
And water
And earth

89. POEM FOR BONNIE

I remember picking up Bonnie
In my Mom's gold '72 Nov
Back in the 80's
Between the University
And the Center of the Arts
And then we went
To the Joe Moran gallery
And looked at some sculptures
By Jeannie Mah

May/2021

BIRDLAND SLIM hopes that when you read his poems
That your mind is filled with purple flowers and a valley
Filled with sun. He hopes only that he may enwrap your
Soul in his heart like the darkness enwraps the moon. He
Wants to be that field of summer wheat flowing in the
sun Of your youth. He only has love in his heart for you
and all The Poetry he ever wrote was written for you.

BIRDLAND SLIM CAN BE REACHED AT THE
EMAIL: brucegame08@gmail.com

9 798839 801547